How to E[barcode] a Social Worker:

The Ultimate Guide

Salary, courses, degrees, masters, training,
job description, careers - all covered

By Denise Jackson

Disclaimer and legal notice

Contents

Introduction 9

Medical/Public Health Social Work 12

    Job Description 12

    School required 13

        Degrees... 13

        Masters 14

        Coursework 14

    Licensing exams required 15

    Examples of jobs in the field................................ 15

        Maggie 15

Substance Abuse Social Work 20

    Job Description 20

    School required 20

        Degrees... 20

        Masters 21

        Coursework 21

    Licensing exams required 22

Examples of jobs in the field................................... 22

Sean... 22

Mental Health Social Work.................................... 30

Job Description 30

School required 31

Degrees.. 31

Masters 31

Coursework 32

Licensing exams required 32

Other training 32

Examples of jobs in the field................................. 33

Allison... 33

Child Welfare Social Work.................................... 39

Job Description 39

School required 39

Degrees.. 39

Masters 40

Other Training... 40

Licensing exams required 41

Examples of jobs in the field................................. 41

    Megan: Adoption Social Worker 41

    Nate: Child Welfare Case Worker 45

    Chloe: Middle School Social Worker 49

Forensic Social Work... 54

    Job Description 54

    School required 54

      Degrees... 54

      Coursework 55

    Licensing exams required 56

    Other training 56

    Examples of jobs in the field............................. 56

    Priscilla and Jonathan....................................... 56

Bonus Section: Five Life Hacks for Social Workers 69

Life Hack #1: Find apps for your phone that can make your life easier. 69

Life Hack #2: Read stories (novels, memoirs, guides) from your field. 71

Life Hack #3: Use ordinary board games in therapy to generate discussion in a non-threatening way. 73

Life Hack #4: Recommend these movies to people when they want to know what you do or start spouting clichés at you. ... 76

Life Hack #5: Create a therapy bag with easy to take along items. 79

Introduction

In the movie *It Takes Two*, Kirstie Alley plays a social worker
who has a special attachment to one of the children in her care in
a group home. She portrays a social worker who cares deeply
about children and goes above and beyond. She fights tooth and
nail to be allowed to adopt the little girl by the end of the movie.
Let's be clear here: this is a kid's movie, and therefore is
presented in a shiny, rose-colored way that won't scar young
children for life. And that is a good thing.

Movies like this can spark something in the children that watch
this movie. Beyond all of the fascination with being an
orphan/switching lives, etc, there is the kernel that is planted for
respect and admiration for the social work profession. Watching
Kirstie Alley play a woman who would do anything for the
children in her care can be comforting and inspiring.

The Oxford English Dictionary defines social work as: "work
carried out by trained personnel with the aim of alleviating the
conditions of those in need of help or welfare."

With such a broad definition, what does that mean? Going back to
the above example of Kirstie Alley in *It Takes Two*, let's apply
the definition and see what it means in that case. The work was
that of a child welfare social worker who was in charge of
children in a group home. She lived with the girls and developed
a deep bond with them. Her goal was always to make the lives of
the children better than the day before. In the movie, the social
worker did this in a number of ways. She listened to the kids
when they needed an ear. She supervised them when they needed
boundaries. And she went above and beyond when one of the
girls was in jeopardy. In the end, she even adopted one of the
girls.

The best way to think about social work is to think about the field as one where you can help people and make a real impact on lives.

In this book, you will find out about five key areas of social work: medical/public health social work, substance abuse social work, mental health social work, child welfare social work (including school social work), and forensic social work.

You will find information on what each job entails, how much you can expect to make, and what educational background is required to obtain each position, as well as examples of people engaged in the profession.

If you have bought this book, you have already asked yourself the most important question: what is it that I want to do with my life that can make a difference in the lives of others? And you came to the answer that the social work profession is the path you'd like to explore further.

Before you begin to read, other questions to ask yourself are what kind of people do you want to work with and help? What strengths do you bring with you? What are areas that you feel lacking in?

Even if you are coming from another field, there are numerous areas where your already honed skills can be applied to social work. People who have an interest in the medical profession might find that they are well-suited to medical social work or substance abuse social work--where the majority of the jobs are found in hospitals and treatment centers.

People who are interested in psychology might find a good fit in the mental health social work field dealing with issues of mental illness and the ramifications in a person's life. If you like children, child welfare social work might be a good fit, either in a school setting or as part of a government or community organization.

If you find the legal field or the judicial system exciting, then you might be interested in the forensic social work field.

Medical/Public Health Social Work

Job Description

Medical social work generally involves jobs in a hospital setting, though it could also include other facilities, such as hospice care. People in this field advocate for patient rights and assist in making decisions based on the best information available to the patient. Someone who chooses this career path can expect long hours, often with an on-call status.

Duties of medical social workers include helping during discharge, making evaluations for chemical dependency, child abuse, or specialty teams, facilitating support groups, and promoting ethical decision making. Choosing medical social work means that a person can make a difference in the lives of the numerous patients they come into contact with. Medical social workers help patients navigate the often confusing world of medical care and advocate for the best interests of the patients.

A person who chooses a degree in medical social work must be well-versed in a number of other areas of social work such as child welfare, substance abuse, and mental health social work fields. Medical social workers often work in close conjunction with these other fields, as medical social workers are often on the front lines in terms of seeing patients. The responsibility of finding patients continued services often falls on medical social workers.

According to *salary.com*, the salary range for a medical social worker is $48,788 to $67,869.

School required

According to the website, *thebestschools.org*, the top five
programs in the United States to earn a Master's degree in Social
Work include the University of Michigan, the University of
Illinois, Washington University in St. Louis, Columbia
University, and the University of Washington.

When choosing a school it is important to consider what kind of
environment the school provides as well as what professors the
school employs. Knowing what area of medical social work
interests you the most can help make the decision easier for you,
as some schools will have a faculty that specializes in one area
over others.

There are many good programs at smaller colleges as well that
can be a good fit for students seeking a more personal connection
to staff and fellow students.

Degrees

Some schools offer a Bachelor's of Social Work, but many
positions in the field require a master's degree as well as
licensure. People with only a BSW will find that while there are
jobs in the field, the scope of duties will be greatly reduced
without an MSW. For example, if a person found a job in a
hospital, their duties might be centered only on things like
discharging patients rather than the full gamut of responsibilities
of someone with a MSW.

Many people find that a good option for themselves is to get their
BSW degree, find a job, and then go back for their MSW. This
choice serves to help with finances while getting the MSW, but
also provides valuable work experience.

13

Masters

Students with a BSW can generally expect to earn some credit toward their MSW and be on a somewhat accelerated course. All MSW programs require a bachelor's degree from an accredited university.

Most of the MSW programs include field work or an internship, though requirements vary depending on the school. Some schools have specific organizations that they work with to determine where students get internships, while others have greater flexibility. Placements for internships in the medical profession can include hospitals or community health organizations.

Coursework

Some sample classes from the University of Michigan's website include Theories and Practices for Community Action and Social Change, Social Problems and Social Work Today, Basic Social Work Research, and Interpersonal Practice with Individuals, Families, and Small Groups.

The Washington University website lists some interesting concentration and specialization choices including American Indian and Alaska Native, Older Adults and Aging Societies, Social Entrepreneurship, and System Dynamics.

Columbia University offers both an on campus, and an online version of its' MSW program.

In all the MSW programs, students are taught a broad range of topics from theory to practice, and most allow students to choose a field of specialization. A person considering the field of medical social work should consider their interests, and where their strengths lie. Taking a diverse course selection before choosing an

14

emphasis can help expose students to the options available for them after graduation.

Licensing exams required

All MSW students are licensed through the Association of Social Work Boards. There are several levels of licensure, and to achieve the highest level a person usually works for several years under supervision.

Here is an example of the state of Texas' licensing page:

> *http://www.dshs.state.tx.us/socialwork/default.shtm*

Other training

Medical social workers can choose to get certificates in further specialized fields such as HIV and AIDS.

Examples of jobs in the field

Maggie

Let's meet Maggie, a recently licensed social worker in the field of medical social work. She has a job at a mid-size hospital in a large town in the Midwest. She's been at the position for over a year and enjoys the diversity that she encounters each day.

Today she gets a text at four-thirty in the morning. She's on call this week, but she managed to get home by ten-thirty the night before so she got to sleep in her own bed. Sometimes she catches a nap at work before the end of her shift.

When she gets in she finds paperwork for a patient on the cardiac floor who is being discharged at six a.m. to go to a rehab facility. She reads through the instructions quickly and heads to the floor to meet with the patient and his family.

She taps softly on the door because she knows that most patients hate being woken up first thing in the morning. Not the case with Mr. Lawrence. He's sitting up in bed, looking tired but happy. Maggie assumes that he's excited to be released even if it is to a rehab facility.

"How are you feeling this morning, Mr. Lawrence?" she asks in the chipper voice she uses during discharge. She's found that if she keeps an upbeat demeanor, the patients are more likely to respond in kind.

"Ready to get out of this place," Mr. Lawrence replies.

"More than ready," echoes a woman sitting beside his bed. She stands and introduces herself as his daughter.

Maggie asks if Mr. Lawrence is okay with his daughter being in the room for his discharge instructions. He agrees. The two begin by discussing his medical transport in an ambulance.

Mr. Lawrence frowns and says, "I thought my daughter would be able to drive me."

Maggie hears the trembling in his voice. She knows that he wants to find some measure of control in this whole situation. Perching on the edge of his bed, Maggie reaches out and takes his hand.

"I know that would be nicer," she says. "But you need to stay hooked up to the IV when you are transported. That's why you need to go in the ambulance."

Mr. Lawrence's frown deepens, but he nods. Maggie finishes the discharge instructions and answers some more of their questions. By the time she's done, she realizes that she famished and fishes a granola bar out of her pocket. She munches on it as she scrolls through her schedule on her phone.

She has to be at a transplant team meeting in twenty minutes, so she has just enough time to work on some paperwork. She types up her notes from her meeting with Mr. Lawrence, and she also works on notes from a few other patients that had been moved to rehab facilities earlier in the week.

She lingers over one that hits home for her. A young woman had been in a fairly horrific car accident. Both of her legs were broken, and one hadn't been able to be saved. The woman would spend the next few months in rehab getting stronger before she could be fitted with a prosthetic. Maggie ran across this feeling occasionally. The one where she could be the patient she was advising. In those moments she felt less than confident. In this particular case, however, the girl's mother had pulled Maggie aside and told her what a difference she had made in the whole hospitalization process--how much Maggie had been their rock in the storm.

Wiping her hands on her pants, she grabs the file folder for the cardiac transplant meeting. She knows she'll have to report on the progress with the insurance company, as well as the support system that is in place for the patient and his wife before, during, and after the transplant. Fortunately she's been through all of this before, but the first time she sat through a transplant team meeting she'd been terrified. She'd felt completely out of her depth.

Maggie never imagined that she would be in this position when she was in college. During her undergraduate years she majored in psychology with no real idea what she wanted to do after college. She happened to land a job in the social work department of a small-town hospital helping with discharge instructions. Her supervisor encouraged her to make as much of the job as she could, and Maggie found that she had a good rapport with both the patients and their families. She made connections with people at local rehab facilities and helped to put a new system into place for patients moving from the hospital to rehab.

After a few years, Maggie decided that she wanted to get her master's degree in Medical Social Work. Her supervisor at the hospital cheered her on and acted as her supervisor for her clinical process during her MSW program. It took her three years while working full time, and she still wants to obtain a few different certificates, but her degree allowed her to move to a bigger hospital with more responsibilities.

The hospital supervisor, Jane, wants Maggie to consider applying for her job as Jane is leaving in about a month. Maggie isn't sure she's ready to run the whole social work department, but she appreciates the vote of support from someone she admires.

At the transplant meeting, Maggie updates the team on the excruciatingly slow process of getting the insurance company to sign off on all the prerequisites for the operation to move forward. Today she's pleased to share that all but one area has been approved. The family support structure has been in place for weeks.

After the meeting, Maggie goes to finish up paperwork and after that she visits with one of the other social workers. She knows how important it is to keep up a good relationship with her co-workers. It's very easy to become isolated in this job, and co-workers are the best allies. The man vents for a while about the impossible behavior of a family during discharge, and Maggie sympathizes. She feels renewed after their visit and sits in her office for a few minutes staring out the window, reflecting on all the positive things that happen during her job. She knows that she feels better when she focuses on the good things.

Substance Abuse Social Work

Job Description

Substance abuse social workers work with those who have chemical substance dependencies to help them overcome their addictions and move down the road toward sobriety. The job requires that the social worker be well-versed in many aspects of social work such as mental health, medical, and education.

A person who chooses a career in substance abuse social work could work in community mental health centers, residential treatment facilities, or many other places. Substance abuse social workers also tend to run community-based education programs aimed at a specific population, so there are many paths within this career.

According to *allpsychologycareers.com*, a substance abuse social worker could expect to make around $41,880.

School required

Degrees

The Dallas County Community College District offers several associate's degrees in applied sciences for substance abuse social work. While these degrees wouldn't allow you the full range of job prospects that lengthier degrees would, all of these options would allow you to get into the workplace within two years. The reality of having job experience could put you in a better position when pursuing a BSW or a MSW.

With most BSW programs, the coursework for the degree program begins after one or two years of general education courses. BSW programs often allow for some degree of personalization based on interest, as most contain several coursework options to fulfill a particular requirement.

Another good option for someone interested in substance abuse social work is to obtain a Bachelor's of Science in Psychology. This degree can be helpful in understanding the psychology behind the behavioral choices of addiction.

Masters

A MSW with an emphasis in substance abuse counseling will allow you to go in depth with your core area of interest. You will also study diagnostic techniques, various counseling methods, and career options that can lead you down different paths.

Someone with a MSW in substance abuse might choose to work with teens in a residential facility, with veterans, or with the homeless population of a certain city. A MSW program can provide you with internship opportunities and connect you with individuals who specialize in your field of interest.

A MSW degree is especially helpful if you are interested in having your own practice, though you would need a specialization in counseling.

Coursework

Examples of courses that a student in a substance abuse social work program might take include topics that cover clinical evaluations, treatment options for different populations, adolescent substance abuse, substance abuse during pregnancy, as well as many others.

Licensing exams required

Other than the state's licensing exam (each state's requirements vary, and you can look them up online), up to 3000 hours of counseling experience are required in the field. After graduation, an additional 100 hours of clinical supervision is also required to be certified by the National Board of Certified Counselors. In addition, the NBCC offers a certificate as a Master Addiction Counselor, which you could achieve in addition to your master's degree.

Examples of jobs in the field

Sean

Sean surveyed the table of snacks and coffee that he'd laid out for the members of his counseling group. This was the fourth session they'd had of the new group, and each week they seemed to dwindle in numbers. He had no idea who would show up today. Hopefully the enticement of hot drinks and a warm room would be enough to draw people in from the January chill.

He was employed by a non-profit organization that helped get homeless veterans off the streets and into government-funded housing programs. Before being eligible, the men and women had to complete a certain number of group counseling sessions for addiction recovery before they could be considered for a spot.

Every seven weeks Sean began the cycle again, offering a new group of people a chance to turn their lives around. He worked hard to keep his head in the right place because often he had more failure than he had success, but when things went well he could see that what he was doing made a difference in the vets' lives.

At ten o'clock, he sat down in the circle of folding chairs he'd set up in the basement of the church that hosted their meetings each week. Sean examined the green and white checked floor tiles while he waited. He felt the familiar tension in his stomach as the clock ticked the seconds by. Finally, he heard the outside metal door clank open and the heavy sound of boots making their way down the stairs to the basement. He let out a sigh of relief as he saw four people who had been at all the previous sessions shuffle into the space, shaking off snow and cold.

After greetings were exchanged and food was taken, Sean invited each person to share their story again, and tell the group how they had been doing over the past week, as well as reiterating what his or her goal was.

Mark Smith went first. He was a burly, older man who had served in the Vietnam War, doing three tours of duty before being unceremoniously dumped back into civilian life. Mark said that he'd thought about going to college, but he had never been book smart, so he'd given up that option early on. Instead he'd tried to become a mechanic, which had worked for a period of time.

He met a young woman who he fell in love with. They dated and eventually married. But he was plagued by PTSD, though he didn't have a name for it back then. Instead he hid the intense nightmares that haunted him at night and the simmering rage that he couldn't explain during the day. He stayed away from home as much as he could. That had led to fights, and he, in turn, began drinking.

After he lost his job at the car shop where he worked, he took to drinking all day, often holed up in his study while his wife went to work. When she confronted him about the escalation of his substance abuse, fighting ensued. Enough that his wife left. Mark never said exactly what happened, but Sean noticed that each time the older man spoke of the incident he choked up.

23

Rather than being a wake-up call, his wife's absence seemed to make Mark spiral out of control faster. Eventually he lost his house, then the apartment he moved into. Being on the street hadn't scared Mark, but the thought that he wouldn't be able to find enough alcohol to numb the nightmares that haunted him was terrifying. He panhandled, and let himself go numb to the world.

He continued that way for years until he nearly froze to death one sub-zero winter's night. A Good Samaritan had gotten him to the emergency department of a local hospital. That was Mark's wake-up call. He spoke to the hospital social worker who had gotten him in touch with Sean. From there, Sean had helped Mark get into a rehab facility through the Veteran's Administration. The VA had also arranged for Sean to be part of Mark's post-rehab care plan.

Sean was pleased to see Mark doing so well, but worried that the older man seemed…slower than he had before, his movements and speech taking longer. That might be a side effect of his medication. Sean made a note to check on that.

The next person to share was also the only woman in the group. She was a soft spoken lady named Rosa, and Sean still had a hard time believing that she needed his help. Rosa's story started when she was graduated college right before 9/11. She had been part of the ROTC group on campus and had started her career as a first grade teacher, serving with her state's army reserve unit on weekends.

When her reserve unit was called to active duty, Rosa was thrilled to have an opportunity to serve. She was trained and put in charge of a tech unit. They shipped out to Iraq. That's when Rosa usually stopped talking. There was clearly more to her story, and Sean had tried every technique he knew to draw the experiences out of her without being pushy. That day he decided to remain silent.

His patience paid off, and eventually Rosa began to talk about seeing a road side bomb detonate on a truck carrying part of her unit. Several of the men were severely injured, and one man had died. She'd developed an anxiety disorder that had its roots in that one experience. Sean actually breathed a sigh of relief. Knowing what had caused Rosa's anxiety disorder allowed him to help her all the more. Often times there was no clear cause, so Sean was grateful that he could offer the woman more assistance.

When she arrived back in her home town, she was shocked to find that life had moved on without her. She was offered a job at her former school district, but she declined, opting instead to move back in with her parents. They were older and experiencing health problems. For Rosa, their neediness allowed her an escape from dealing with her own problems. Her mother died unexpectedly only three months after her discharge. The loss sent Rosa into a tailspin.

She got her father into an assisted-living facility, sold the house and belongings, and decided to travel the country. Rosa told the group that she could see that she was trying to run away from her demons, but they pursued her wherever she went. Like Mark, Rosa began drinking heavily. Her money ran out on the other side of the country. Rosa had begged an aunt to help her get home.

When she'd returned to her home town, she found that yet again, life had moved on. She had nowhere to stay, occasionally finding a bed at the local women's shelter, but more often than not, she crashed wherever she landed. She trolled bars looking for men to buy her drinks. Often times she would end up being kicked out of bars because, as she said, she was a belligerent drunk.

Rosa hadn't had the sort of wake-up call that Mark had had. Instead her resolve had come from the persistent concern of her father who continued to reach out to her despite his own failing health. He asked her to go to a rehab facility for him, so that they could spend whatever time he had left together. She went grudgingly.

Mark made a note to talk to Rosa after the group session was over, and see if there was anything he could do to support her father as well. He knew that if he could expand her support network, then she had a much better chance at success.

Paul O'Donnell went next. He was the sort of guy Sean would have avoided during high school. Paul was the sort of guy who would have bullied Sean, and occasionally the social worker found his prejudice clouding his vision about Paul. One of his professors in grad school had warned him and his classmates time and again that being self-aware was one of the most important traits a good substance abuse social worker could have.

Paul had gone into the Air Force right after high school with the intent of flying planes. That was all he'd ever wanted to do, but other than the military he had no means to pursue that goal. He loved everything about the Air Force and discovered that he could have a great career after he was discharged as an air traffic controller.

He married his high school sweetheart before his deployment. While he was overseas, she found out that she was pregnant. Things seemed to be going well for Paul. He served two tours of duty and seemed to return unscathed from both. By the time he was discharged, Paul and his wife had two children, and he'd logged hours and hours of flight time. He'd completed his training to be an air traffic controller and had a job lined up and waiting for him when he got home.

Adjusting to civilian life was harder than he'd expected. No one, not even his wife, understood the difference, and he started to withdraw from those around him. He still functioned on an everyday level, but he began seeking out other vets who had served around the same time.

One of his new buddies—a man named Stu—smoked a lot of weed. Paul started smoking too. He didn't see it as a big deal. When he hung out at Stu's apartment, they'd get stoned and play video games. Paul said that he didn't realize how much time he was spending at Stu's place until his wife kicked him out. At first Paul had been furious, but he'd assumed that he'd just crash at Stu's or another friend's place. That didn't last long. Soon, Paul found himself bouncing from motel to motel.

He also had a problem at work when he failed a drug test. Fortunately his employer had issued him a warning, and put him on paid leave so he could get help. Paul's wife had made the separation legal, but he said she seemed willing to work things out if he could get his life together.

Sean admired Paul's quiet resolve and humility, but he often wondered if he was also harder on the other man because of his own prejudices. Sean knew that he'd have to look over Paul's paperwork and make any adjustments that were needed.

The last member of the group to be back was the one who surprised Sean the most. Luther Martin had served in Vietnam like Mark, but he had been into heavy drugs before he was drafted. He smoked pot while he was serving, and continued the heavy drug use after he returned.

His parents kicked him out shortly after he was discharged, and he was almost immediately on the streets. He moved to a bigger city and panhandled to get money for food. To get his drugs, he became a dealer. Occasionally he would break into homes for some quick cash. He'd been in and out of jail his whole life.

The last time he was arrested, he was sent to the state penitentiary for three years for a petty theft. He found a way to deal while he was in jail, and right before his release he was caught. The judge who oversaw his case should have sentenced him to longer jail time. However, Luther had cirrhosis of the liver, and the judge was known for creative solutions. Luther was sent to an intensive rehab facility.

Sean knew that he needed to touch base with Luther's medical team. The other man had mentioned briefly that he was being considered for a liver transplant, but his team wanted to make sure he had his life on the right track before they recommended anything.

Luther often seemed sad that he'd ended up where he was, but he never took responsibility for his choices. He often blamed a myriad of people in the same breath. He was by turns morose and belligerent, and he was often the one who interrupted the other members of the group to make snarky comments. Sean had a hard time reining him in at those moments. Other times Luther offered support, especially when he commiserated with Mark about their time in Vietnam.

Sean ended the session by having each person reiterate their goals. Mark wanted to get into a stable place so he could change the course of the rest of his life. He intensely desired being able to get his PTSD under control. Rosa wanted to get well for her father. She was vague about any other ambitions, but Sean knew that he would try to get her to open up farther in coming sessions. Paul wanted to clean up his life so he could reunite with his wife and children and keep his job. Luther wanted a new liver.

As the group members lingered over coffee and food, Sean made notes and moved to speak one on one with each person. He touched base with Mark and gave him an encouraging review. When he asked Rosa if there was any way he could help get more support for her father, the woman began to cry. She was having trouble getting him his benefits, and if he couldn't stay in assisted living she didn't know where he would go. Sean promised to set up an appointment for her with a member of his non-profit who could walk her through the paperwork.

Paul shrugged off Sean's attempt at conversation, and it was all Sean could do to remind himself that the other man was just using a coping mechanism. The reaction wasn't personal. Sean reiterated his help was available if Paul needed anything. For one moment Paul looked up from his coffee cup, and with his jaw clenched, gave one quick nod.

Luther needed Sean to talk to the head of his transplant team so they could move to the next phase. Sean promised to do what he could. Luther's face contorted like he might begin to cry, but the moment passed as he turned back to the table to spread cream cheese on a bagel.

As the group left, Sean cleaned up the session, putting away folding chairs and washing dishes in the church's tiny kitchen. When everything was taken care of, he gathered his files to head back to his office. He had to write up his notes from the therapy session, review each client's file, make the appropriate phone calls, and prepare for the next week's session. Though the therapy group was only one part of his job, he found it the most challenging and rewarding part.

Mental Health Social Work

Job Description

A mental health social worker works with people with mental illness and their families. They assess individuals at risk for mental illness, and help their clients find services within the community. Mental health social workers collaborate with a team of individuals that often includes psychiatrists, psychologists, and therapists or counselors. Mental health social workers may also work with staff in hospitals or treatment facilities.

Mental health social workers also help their clients with their daily needs. The social worker might help her client obtain employment or secure insurance. Clients might need to have their social worker guide them to sources for education on mental illness and treatment options. The social worker might also help his client's family obtain services to expand the client's support network.

A person interested in the mental health social work field needs to be committed to finding the best care possible for their clients, and thus needs to have a broad knowledge of all areas of social work. Clients can range in age from children to the elderly, and with each age group comes different needs. Mental health social workers work in a variety of settings including hospitals, treatment facilities, schools, and community health programs.

The average salary for a person in this field is around $51,000.

School required

Degrees

Like other fields in social work, a bachelor's in social work or a related field is the first step. A master's degree is preferred for many positions. People interested in this field need an extensive education to give them broad knowledge with which to deal with the issues that the mental health profession presents.

Masters

The School of Social Work at the University of Michigan offers a unique master's degree program with a mental health concentration. They allow students who have earned a bachelor's degree in social work to earn credit for that degree that can count toward hours in their master's degree program. They also have an extended degree program that can stretch out the program for people who are already working.

If students wish to complete their master's degree program quickly, the University of Michigan offers an option that allows students to get their MSW in one year. The program begins in September for the fall semester, includes a winter semester and a spring semester, and concludes with graduation during the following summer.

Another unique feature of the program is that they feature a component that allows students to partner with the Peace Corps if they are interested in an international component as well as one working with children. This piece includes a twenty-seven month commitment to serve with the Peace Corps.

Coursework

The social work program at the University of Southern California offers a concentration in mental health social work. Courses that are offered as part of the concentration include human development and mental health, evaluation of research, and clinical practice in mental health settings.

Each of these courses, as well as all the others in the program, is designed to give students a chance to hone their skills while getting their social work degree. The courses allow students to prepare for the challenges they will face in their field, while giving them resources to make their career path smoother.

Social work programs include a clinical experience or an internship. For the mental health field, a person might be placed in a hospital or a community health center. Other areas might include being in an internship position in a job that the student already has, and is supervised in the position. Each program has different requirements, and it is important for the student to check into each program thoroughly.

Licensing exams required

Licensing exams vary by state, so it is important to know your state's requirements, but generally each state requires a comprehensive exam as well as some hours of supervision under the guidance of a licensed social worker.

Other training

Many programs allow students to choose a sub-concentration or an additional certificate that gives the student knowledge that can help when choosing a career path. Examples of this for the mental health profession include veterans, gerontology, and children.

Examples of jobs in the field

Allison

When she wrote her essay for college during the summer before her senior year in high school, Allison knew exactly what she wanted to do with her life. Her mother had suffered from severe depression for years. There were parts of her childhood that Allison couldn't remember her mother being part of because there were long stretches of time when her mother couldn't even get out of bed.

During her sixth-grade year, her father knew that he either needed to get her mother help or the family was going to fall apart. He called the local community mental health center, and they connected him with an amazing social worker who changed everything. She demystified depression and had made the whole family feel like the stigma of mental illness wasn't that bad.

The social worker had gotten Allison into a therapy group for children of parents with mental illness. Allison had found a safe place to discuss her feelings. After her mother got out of her treatment program, their social worker had continued to follow up with the family for years. They had all continued to do well, but Allison knew that things could have been vastly different if not for their social worker. She wanted to do that with her life. She wanted to help save families.

She had been accepted to her first choice social work program and had studied hard. Sometimes she felt like her classmates in the program didn't understand her motivation or drive, but she didn't care. She knew what her ultimate goal was, and she didn't care how long it took her to get there.

For grad school, she had chosen an accelerated program with a concentration in mental health social work. Once she finished her degree, she had jumped right into her field, getting a job in a community mental health center just like the one that had helped her family when she was young.

With her drive, Allison was able to get an internship at a community mental health center working with elderly and home bound patients. The bulk of her job as an intern was to do intake surveys for depression risk. At first she felt shaky even when she was in her training phase. She knew that she was doing the same thing that the social worker had done for her family so many years ago. It made her feel out of her depth, and she even questioned her career decision.

As she worked out her system, however, she was able to connect with her clients. When she was welcomed into their homes and sat with them, asking them the questions on the mental health questionnaire that the mental health center used to assess the depression risk, she found their stories eerily similar to her mother's. When she began to share the bare bones of her mother's story, she noticed that her clients began to open up to her.

Her internship sparked an interest in gerontology, and she found an online school that offered a certificate that she could work on at the same time as her master's degree. The more she learned about the gerontology field, the more she was certain that she wanted to work with an aging population.

The woman who served as her supervisor during her internship made Allison feel like her decision to work with the elderly was the right choice, and gave her continued and expanded duties over the year that Allison worked with the agency.

One of the parts of her internship that Allison had not expected was how many gaps in care she discovered when she spoke with her clients. She was baffled by the lack of respect and dignity that seemed to be absent from these people's lives, especially those living in assisted-care facilities.

During one master's class seminar, her professor assigned the class a paper that became like a thesis for Allison. She interviewed dozens of residents in assisted-living facilities in the general area, compiled the information in a way that highlighted the gaps in care, and then she wrote a plan to fill those gaps. Her professor had been so impressed with her initiative that he put her in touch with an elderly rights lobbyist group.

When Allison was contacted by them, she found that her passion exploded. Her drive went into hyper gear, and as she graduated, she knew that she had to do everything she could to make a difference for the aging population.

Immediately after graduation Allison accepted a job with a non-profit group that defended residents in assisted-living facilities and nursing homes when allegations of elder abuse arose. She joined a team of lawyers, health care workers, and social workers. She continued to do patient assessments during the initial team visit after a claim was filed. Each time she went with the group that always included a lawyer, a nurse, and a social worker, she assured herself that she wouldn't be shocked by what she saw. The truth was that she was shocked time and again.

After each meeting with a new client, she continued to ask herself if what she was doing was the most beneficial use of her time. Occasionally she felt like she should pursue a different direction, but she wasn't sure where she would head, and she still felt like she wanted to work in gerontology.

Allison worked for the non-profit for four years before she burnt out. One day after she served on a team that went to meet with a woman in a nursing home and her family who had filed a neglect report when they discovered infected bed sores. Allison had seen more than her share of bed-sore neglect cases, but she'd never seen a case like that. The woman's entire left side was basically one open sore with festering pus everywhere. The smell alone was enough to turn her stomach. She had no idea how anyone could treat another human being this way.

That night she sobbed to her mother over the phone. She felt like she needed to quit right away. The question that she kept asking her mother over and over again was: Had she made any difference in all the work she'd done over the past four years?

Her mother reminded her of the social worker who had helped their family. The woman hadn't come in to fix everything that was wrong; she had come in to support them while pointing them in the right direction to get treatment and help. She reassured Allison that she had done that and more in the past four years, and she would continue to do it for years to come. But, her mother said, maybe it was time for Allison to pursue another avenue for the sake of her own mental health.

Allison quit her job the next day. Her boss had been disappointed but sympathetic. With the yawning chasm of time before her, Allison took a trip to clear her head. While she was away, she did something she'd never done before and climbed a mountain. It was a small mountain, but she would always credit it with helping her get a new focus in her life.

When she came down from the mountain she knew that she was going back to school. This time she was going to get her certificate in at least one other area of social work as well as get an MBA so she could run an assisted-living facility.

The next few years were grueling. She worked odd jobs so that she could go full time for her MBA degree, while obtaining her certificate in forensic social work online. After she'd completed her certificate, she decided to get her CNA degree so that she could understand the medical side of her new goal.

All the important people in her life—her parents, friends, boyfriend, professors—supported her, but constantly told her to be careful not to burn herself out again. But this time Allison knew what she was doing. She knew that she was going to become the head of one of the facilities that had had the worst abuse allegations filed, and she was going to turn the place around. That's how she was going to make a difference.

When Allison graduated, she got a job as an assistant director of a small assisted- living facility. The place was idyll in terms of the care they provided. They had enough CNAs that each resident got plenty of medical attention, and the food was amazing. The activities director had social events planned morning, noon, and night.

There was a greenhouse that was used year round, and the facility had several pets that belonged to all the residents. Two dogs and a cat roamed the hallways, visiting those who had their doors open. Birds were kept in the common areas and drew people in with their bright colors and energetic attitudes. Allison took in everything she could about what was being done well, and kept her eyes open for job positions at the facilities she knew needed her the most.

Eventually a director position came open at one of the places she wanted to be at. She applied, and she got the job. Immediately she took an assessment of what was going on, and she began to implement changes. She gathered the nurses and CNAs together her first day on the job. She laid out her expectations and the changes that would be made, including the consequences for not following the rules. She told all of them that if they couldn't get on board, then they needed to leave immediately. Five people quit.

Over the next few months, Allison worked to assess the mental health of each resident, often doing the assessments herself. She knew that those most at risk of depression—or already suffering from depression or anxiety—were at far greater risk of being abused.

It took her years to turn the facility around, but Allison firmly believed in what she was doing. She dug her heels in and worked hard. Slowly but surely, the facility became the kind of place she'd envisioned, and the mental health of her residents improved by leaps and bounds. She continued to engage with other social workers to continually ensure that they were using best practices, and all the hard work clearly paid off in the health and well-being of her residents.

Child Welfare Social Work

Job Description

This is about working with families who have problems in order to protect the children. The children could be facing many different issues including abuse , medical or abandonment.

The median salary for a child welfare social worker is $43000, though that number does depend heavily on where one works.

School required

Degrees

A bachelor's degree is required for most child welfare social work positions. *Socialworkdegreesonline.com* estimates that nearly one third of child welfare workers have a bachelor's degree specifically in child welfare social work. The rest of child welfare social workers typically have a degree in a related field, such as psychology. Degrees in sociology or even child development can be useful in the child welfare social work field because the information that a person studies in these fields inform him or her about the basics in child development, which is particularly useful when assessing a child.

Aurora.edu offers an online bachelor's degree in social work. The program includes coursework in areas such as social work in communities, families and individuals, and development over the lifespan. There is also a field work component to the degree.

The benefit of an online degree program is that students can continue to work while taking classes at their own pace. The *Aurora.edu* program offers a comprehensive program that would be a good foundation for any area of social work, but child welfare social work in particular because when one deals with children, they also must deal with the family unit, so the child welfare social worker must be well-versed in all forms of social work.

Students in a program like *Aurora.edu* are often eligible to take state licensing exams, which can give a student advanced standing when applying to master's degree programs. This means that a student is given credits for the degree already earned; meaning that less time will have to be spent on the master's degree. Most states also require students to take a licensing exam to become child welfare social workers.

No matter what degree program a student chooses, he or she must consider future goals and how the school he or she attends will impact those goals.

Masters

While a master's degree in social work is not generally required for people interested in child welfare social work, a listing for the Louisiana Department of Child and Family Services illustrates how beneficial a master's degree in social work can be. The job posting states that the salary range for hires in the state of Louisiana ranges from $2,825.00-$5,945.00 monthly, based on the level of education one has.

Other Training

The University of Pittsburgh's School of Social Work offers a special certificate in Child, Youth, and Families. Coursework includes Child and Families at Risk, and Child and Family Policy, as well as internships working with at-risk populations.

A certificate such as this is useful for social workers with degrees or concentrations in other areas if they are interested in expanding their field of expertise.

Licensing exams required

Each state requires people interested in child welfare social work to pass a licensing exam, and school social work may require other licensure depending upon the state.

Examples of jobs in the field

In this section you will meet three social workers who fall under the title of child welfare and school social work. Megan works for a private religious-based organization as an adoption social worker. Nate works for a state child welfare department as a child welfare case worker. And Chloe works for a school district in a middle school serving grades six to eight. There are several similarities to their stories, including their commitment to children, but there are also several significant differences.

Megan: Adoption Social Worker

When Megan began at the private organization she works for, she truly believed in the mission of uniting children with families. This belief helped her build a strong rapport with the families she served. Her responsibilities stemmed primarily from two areas in the field. One was helping birth mothers connect with families interested in domestic infant adoption. The other was helping families who were interested in adopting overseas wade through the lengthy process. Over the past six years she has seen numerous adoptions succeed and numerous adoptions fall through. Her belief that uniting children and families is still intact, though she has a more realistic view of the pain that comes from the loss associated with adoption.

Two cases stand out for her as the most important of her career because they showed her how and where she needed to grow to become a better social worker.

The first involved a birth mother who came into the agency soon after Megan was hired. The girl was young—fourteen—and scared. She glommed on to Megan with a fierceness that Megan found endearing. Against the advice of her colleagues, Megan allowed herself to get attached to the girl. She spent hours screening potential families, often feeling like she was choosing them for herself, or for her niece as she often referred to the girl's baby.

Megan justified the sisterly relationship as part of her job. She needed to connect with her clients. But she found that potential families were becoming less and less desirable. Once or twice Megan had found herself thinking that she should offer to adopt the baby. That way the girl could stay involved in both their lives. Ultimately she rejected that idea because she knew she wasn't ready to be a parent.

Finally Megan found a family that was perfect. She presented them to the girl, who trusted Megan's judgment. When the family met the girl, they embraced her wholeheartedly, and Megan felt twinges of jealousy. Suddenly the girl didn't need her as much, and Megan felt lost. She pushed her way into meetings between the two parties, justifying yet again that it was her job to protect both sides. And to protect them, she needed to be involved.

Eventually the girl gave birth, and the baby boy was handed over to his new family. In the twenty-four hours that followed the birth, Megan sat with the girl, dozing at her bedside. She watched this girl, who was a child herself, cradle her baby. Halfway through that day, the girl began to talk about changing her mind. The family who was set to adopt the baby was clearly devastated, but they put on a brave face, and allowed Megan to do her job. When they stepped out of the room, Megan felt the crush of all the things she had done wrong over the past five months. It hit her squarely in the chest. She knew that she needed to be a professional, and not let her deep attachment to the situation get in the way. Her actual job, she realized, was to help all parties involved to obtain the best possible outcome for all involved.

The girl and Megan had a long talk about the realities of the girl keeping the baby. Megan presented the options that were available to the girl in terms of government assistance, and she promised that she'd find the girl a new social worker. When the girl seemed surprised that Megan wouldn't continue to be with her in any professional capacity, Megan realized yet again that she had let herself get in too deep.

Ultimately the girl chose to give her son to his new family. Megan closed the case file and moved on professionally, but she never forgot them. She learned that she needed to keep a professional distance even if she did feel a personal connection.

The other case that changed her was an international adoption that had gone well from the beginning. The family had been matched with a toddler girl, just fifteen months old, in the country they had chosen, and all the paperwork had moved swiftly. The family had traveled to finalize the adoption, which also went well, when suddenly diplomatic relations between the US and the country of origin stalled. The family was unable to get the exit visa they needed for their daughter in order to bring her back to the United States.

Megan took their frantic call in the middle of the night. At first she was stunned into inaction. This wasn't a case she had ever worried about. Things had gone so smoothly that she had

43

assumed that it was fated, meant to be. It was only her third international adoption, so she still felt out of her depth. She hung up with the family promising to get them answers as soon as she could.

After an emergency call to her supervisor, Megan knew that she was going to have to do some research. She turned to adoption blogs and message boards to find stories similar to what her clients were experiencing. There were several that she found that had been resolved in different ways, and she soaked up as much information as she could.

She began to make calls as soon as she got off the computer. She called the embassy in the country in question. After alerting them to the family's situation, she was given the name and contact number to pass on to the family. She called them immediately, and gave them the information. Then she went back to work. With each call she made she connected with one more person who was willing to help the family.

By the time she got off the phone with a non-profit group in the country who had agreed to provide the family with temporary housing, it was mid-morning. Megan decided it was time to call all the lawmakers in their state. She began with state lawmakers, and moved all the way up to their senators. By the time she was dialing the last number she had begun to feel discouraged. Every office she had called thus far had told her to leave a message.

She gave her spiel to the woman who answered the phone, and to her surprise the woman put her straight through to the senator. After Megan had gotten over her shock of speaking to him, she managed to explain the situation in detail. The senator had been concerned, and promised her that he would look into the matter and call her back.

Megan called the family back. They were overwhelmed by the amount of information she was able to give them, and exhausted from dealing with the bureaucracy of it all. Megan didn't tell them about her call to the senator because she didn't want to give them false hope.

She headed into her office, and jumped every time the phone rang. Finally, toward the end of the day, she had begun to give up hope herself. As she left the office, her cell phone buzzed. It was a call from the senator's office. After a day of political wrangling and haggling, somehow the senator had managed to obtain the exit visa for the family's little girl.

Megan called the family right away, waking them in the middle of the night. She wasn't sure if she made any sense, but somehow she managed to convey the news, and the family was overjoyed. The senator enjoyed some good PR when the family returned, and Megan learned that she was willing to go to extraordinary lengths to help her clients.

Nate: Child Welfare Case Worker

Nate was a child in foster care. He and his two brothers were taken from their parents when they were quite young. Nate, the oldest at eight, was the only one who really remembered their life with their parents. Even those memories grew hazy for him as he grew older.

What he remembered were the days he'd have to scavenge for food when the refrigerator was bare. He remembered always being dirty, and the kids at school teasing him that he smelled. He loved his parents, but he remembered always being angry at them that they couldn't act like grown-ups. None of the other kids his age had to worry about their parents like he did, and he always thought that was unfair.

45

He remembered feeling relief when the social worker showed up and took them to their first foster home. It was a temporary placement, but he got clean clothes, a bath, and a hot meal. He says that memory is what sustains him when he is tasked with removing children from a home.

At first the goal for Nate and his brothers was reunification. When it became clear that his parents weren't going to get their act together, the goal became adoption. The problem then became that there weren't many families willing to adopt three boys, one of whom was almost a teenager. So the three of them were split up. Both of his younger brothers were adopted, but Nate continued to bounce from foster home to foster home.

By the time he was sixteen, Nate had lost count of how many foster homes he'd been a part of. Then his circumstances changed. He landed in a foster home with an older couple whose children had all grown up and left the house. They wanted to adopt him, and he readily agreed. He liked them, and he could see a different future for himself.

When he started college, he found an interest in social work. His classmates, and even a few professors, who knew his story asked him if he wanted to follow in the footsteps of one of his caseworkers. His honest reply was always that he could only remember one or two of his caseworkers, the rest had simply been nameless versions of each other.

Nate began working for a state child welfare agency soon after graduation as a child welfare case worker. His job was to investigate claims of abuse or neglect that were thought to have substantial evidence for a case from the child abuse hotline. He found that he held his breath as he approached each door to ring the bell. His guiding hope was always that the claim had been made in error, and what he would find was a happy home. That did happen from time to time. He learned that often in cases of child custody disputes, the injured party often made claims in anger in hopes of swaying a custody case. It never worked out that way.

When he came to a house where there was obvious neglect, he flashed back to his own childhood. Rather than give him an advantage, his past often hindered him. His anger would often come out in ways that got him reprimanded by his supervisor. Nate couldn't help it, though. He didn't understand how the parents could neglect the very basic needs of their children.

Once when he entered a house filled with dog feces and garbage, he'd screamed himself hoarse as the drunk mother stared up at him in confusion. The three children had hidden in fear. After getting chewed out by his supervisor, Nate realized that he had every right to be angry—who wouldn't be under the circumstances?—but he could never allow that anger to show.

When he removed children after that incident, he made sure that he told them exactly what was going on, even in the midst of chaos. Sometimes the parents realized what was happening and became frantic. The police often had to get involved in those situations. Even then, Nate made sure that he explained everything in a calm, even tone. Keeping the kids in the dark served no purpose for anyone.

Nate was also a strong believer in allowing children to take at least one familiar thing with them. He knew plenty of workers who were more concerned with removing the children from the home as quickly as possible, but Nate remembered the awful feeling of waking up the next morning with nothing of his own. If things were truly dangerous for the children, the police were always involved anyway. He didn't see the harm in taking the children into their room to get one special thing. Even through the fear and confusion, Nate could see the gratitude in their eyes.

One of the most heartbreaking cases he'd encountered was that of a little girl who had been beaten by her step-father until both her arms were fractured. The hospital, as a mandated reporter, had called the hotline and filed a report. Nate had gone the next morning to find the girl with two temporary casts and a face full of darkening bruises. There was a contusion over her left eye that had also received several stitches. The police accompanied Nate and arrested both the mother and the step-father.

The little girl didn't say a word as her parents were led away, but tears streamed silently down her cheeks. Nate had done his best to explain to her what was happening, but he wasn't sure if the little girl understood or was listening to anything he said. When he told her that she could take a few special things, she stopped crying a bit. He offered to help her, but she shook her head.

Nate followed her around the apartment as she took her school backpack and added four things. The first was a ratty teddy bear that had been lying on her unmade bed. Even as she struggled with her casts, he allowed her to do it by herself. If he was taking her from everything she knew, the least he could do was allow her the autonomy to get what she needed.

Then they went into her mother's room. The little girl very carefully picked up a flannel nightgown from the floor, and tucked it into her backpack. She also grabbed at a small perfume bottle on the top of her mother's dresser. After knocking over several things, the little girl finally managed to grab the bottle and get it into her backpack. Finally she pointed to a picture in the living room of herself and her mother, and asked Nate to put it in her bag.

As they were leaving the apartment with her backpack and a small suitcase of clothes, the little girl had remarked to him that she just wanted something to remember her mother by. Nate didn't know how she knew that her mother would never be reunited with her because the goal would be reunification only if the step-father got out of the picture, but he knew that life was never so simple.

The case stayed with him even after he found a foster family who wanted to adopt the girl, and another worker took over the case. He reflected on how intuitive children were, and how as he looked back he had known so much more than the adults in his life had been willing to tell him.

He resolved to continue to provide as much information to his young clients as he could and fight for them no matter what the circumstances. He also began to share more of his past with his clients, which he found put them at ease. His anger never subsided, but he learned how to channel it into more productive ways.

Chloe: Middle School Social Worker

6:45 a.m.: Chloe gets to school, and heads straight to the teacher's lounge to make coffee. She's often the first one in, and she likes the quiet that the morning provides her before the school explodes in noise and the barely controlled chaos that is a middle school.

She has also discovered that the early morning in the teacher's lounge is the best place to get the best gossip that the teacher's trade on the students. At first she was shocked by the amount of information and speculation that the teachers shared with one another, but she had come to appreciate the bits of news. It helped her when she called students in that she'd never met. In a school of nearly seven hundred students, every personal item helped her connect with the kids she worked with.

8:00 a.m.: The students begin to arrive with the first load of buses. During warmer weather, students waited in the courtyard,

49

but in the winter months they gathered in the cafeteria until the bell rang dismissing them to their lockers.

The rain that morning means that the students will be waiting just steps from her office. She knows the noise level will soon be overwhelming, but she keeps her door wide open. More than once a student has wandered in to chat.

8:15 a.m.: Sure enough, a student comes to her door tentatively, wavering. Chloe greets the girl and invites her to take a seat and grab a piece of candy. The offer of a sugary treat is enough to get the girl to sit down. As soon as she stuffs the chocolate into her mouth, tears pool in the corners of her eyes, and the girl blurts out that her dad was just diagnosed with cancer.

Chloe knows that she'll need more than fifteen minutes with the girl, so she gets the girl's name and homeroom teacher so she can call the office. After she lets the attendance office know that the girl will be in her office for a while that morning she gets back to business.

After listening to all of the girl's fears, Chloe helps her think of ways she could help her father while he was undergoing treatment. Chloe also finds a support group that meets after school at a nearby church. There the girl can meet with other kids her own age who also have parents with cancer.

By the time the girl leaves, she looks relieved. Chloe feels the boost of confidence that she always gets when she helps a student.

9:30 a.m.: Chloe gathers her material to attend an IEP meeting with one of the special education teachers. Her presence at the meeting today is more perfunctory since the team has already identified services that the student needs, and the school has obtained them. Today's meeting is a follow up.

50

9:45 a.m.: One of the student's parents brings up some concerns they are having at home, and the team begins to discuss possible solutions. Chloe remembers a new program at a school across town, and excuses herself to call the coordinator.

When she returns she reports on what the other school has implemented and suggests ways that they can take the same steps at their school.

10:30 a.m.: Today Chloe has lunch room duty, so she eats a quick lunch. While she supervises the first round of students as they each lunch, she chats with the teacher on duty with her. She learns that the other woman is going through a messy divorce and both of her kids grades have been falling. Chloe suggests that she send them to the after-school support group for kids of divorce that Chloe runs. The teacher is grateful and hugs Chloe before the lunch period ends.

12:00 p.m.: Chloe has a meeting with a student who has been having disciplinary problems. The boy slumps down into the chair across from Chloe's desk after helping himself to a handful of candy.

She's dealt with surly students before, but this boy seems to want to make a point about how angry he is at the world. When she asks him if he knows why he's there, he kicks the front of her desk, making a good, metallic reverberating sound. He swears at her, but doesn't answer her question.

Chloe carefully lays out what the problems have been, pausing frequently to make sure that the boy is actually listening. After she gets through the laundry list, the boy swears at her again. She sighs and knows that she's not getting through to him. Then he says something about there not being a point. No one cares about him anyway. Not his parents. Not his foster parents. As he continues on with his list of all the people who have wronged

51

him, Chloe realizes that she's just heard the one bit of information that will at least help her get this boy the services he needs.

After sending him back to class, she heads to the attendance office to get the name of the boy's social worker. She gives the woman a call and makes notes about the various aspects of the boy's life that they can work on at school.

2:00 p.m.: In a rare lull during the day, Chloe heads to the library to help with tutoring. She enjoys these days when she can interact with the students in a way that helps them trust her, but also helps them see her in a role other than school counselor. She never tells them that she's a social worker. Early on in her career, she learned that the label *social worker* had negative associations for students who had been part of the system.

After helping a boy with his pre-algebra, Chloe roams through the stacks, hunting up books that have social themes pertinent to her middle-school charges. She runs a book club that meets at the end of the school day once a week. On her way back from the library, she realizes that the book club meets today. She hustles back to her office.

3:00 p.m.: To be part of her book club, a student must be in advanced language arts and have been on the honor roll every semester. Currently there are seven students that have opted to be in her book club. Each month they read a book with a social issue and meet to discuss it each week.

This week they are starting a new book, and she wants to talk about the issue of bullying before they begin reading. She knows that the discussion will serve two purposes. One, it will introduce a rather serious topic and two, it will let her gauge how well the school is doing at curbing bullying. They started a zero tolerance initiative the year before, and she hopes that it's working.

3:30 p.m.: The book club went well, but Chloe is dismayed to learn that it seems the anti-bullying initiative isn't going as well as they had all hoped. She shakes off the disappointment to get ready for the group she hosts after school for kids of divorce.

The group is fluid and sometimes only two or three students show up, but today there are fifteen. After they eat a snack, they all sit down to share about their family situations. The first few kids have had their parents separated for quite a while, and the last few kids to go have parents that are just separating.

4:30 p.m.: Chloe finishes up some paperwork before she heads home. She's tired, but glad that the day held more good things than bad. She knows that she has more of the good days, and that makes her feel like she's making a difference, even if the progress seems slow or non-existent some days. She knows that she'll never get bored, and even if she helps just one student a day, it is all worth it.

Forensic Social Work

Job Description

Forensic Social workers provide education, counseling, and training for those in the legal system such as lawyers, law enforcement personnel, and people in the correctional system. People who work in this field will often work closely with social workers in other fields.

Those who chose the forensic social work profession might work in clinics or psychiatric hospitals with criminal cases where defendants need evaluation for competency to stand trial. Forensic social workers might also work in the justice system with legal cases involving abuse, termination of parental rights, or even child custody cases. Social workers are also needed during both juvenile and adult court cases where they help defendants navigate the complex legal system

A person who chooses forensic social work can expect a median salary of $39,000. As with other areas of social work, the level of pay is commensurate with the level of education one has.

School required

Degrees

Most people who become forensic social workers get either a bachelor's or a master's degree in social work before pursuing a certificate in forensic social work. There are numerous schools that offer general degrees in social work. The following are three options in various states:

The University of Minnesota's School of Social Work offers a general degree in social work with minors in youth, violence, or family studies. All the minors work well with a forensic social work certificate, as these areas are often involved in the job of a forensic social worker.

The College of Social Work at the University of South Carolina offers numerous options for students seeking social work degrees, including dual enrollment master's programs with public health or law, offering students interested in forensic social work the opportunity to expand their education.

University of Southern California offers a social work master's degree program both on campus and online. There are areas of concentration in adults and healthy aging, children, youth and families, and community and business involvement. They also offer dual degrees in some of the following fields: law, MBA, gerontology, public health, as well as several others.

Coursework

According to a certificate program offered through the Forensic Training Institute, coursework includes forensic practice in the following fields: juvenile and adult criminal justice, mental health, substance abuse, child welfare, education, and family and social services. There is also coursework in diversity training and interviewing victims.

While the above mentioned coursework is specific to that program, the courses offered cover much of the same material as other certification programs. The intent of all the programs is to allow the person being certified to get a broad view of issues they might encounter in the legal system, and how to deal with said issues.

55

Licensing exams required

According to the American Board of Forensic Social Work, to become certified as a forensic social worker a person is required to hold at least a bachelor's degree or higher in social work, be a member of the American College of Forensic Examiners Institute, score one hundred points or higher in a combination of experience, training, education, and other areas. One must also submit the appropriate documentation of diplomas, resumes, etc.

Other training

While any social worker might be called on to be part of the legal system given a particular client's needs, those who specifically choose the forensic social work field benefit hugely from detailed training in the legal field. Knowledge of the laws that pertain to specific areas of clients' cases as well as intimate knowledge of detailed diagnostic criteria serve the forensic social worker well when they must present their testimony to a court. If a social worker in another field wishes to get in to the forensic social work profession, there are certificates available as discussed above, but there is also a benefit from taking legal courses during a master's or bachelor's degree program that can supplement any social work degree.

Examples of jobs in the field

Priscilla and Jonathan

Priscilla and Jonathan work for a non-profit organization as forensic social workers. The following question and answer session helps to get a better view of what a forensic social worker does.

Q. What exactly is a forensic social worker?

Priscilla: In my opinion, I'd define a forensic social worker as someone who works in the legal field in the capacity of a social worker. The legal field includes working with lawyers and other social workers, as well as clients who are part of the legal system.

People who are going through the judicial system need a voice, and that's where forensic social workers come in. I believe it's the job of a forensic social worker to make sure that people in at-risk populations don't fall through the cracks.

Forensic social workers also have an obligation to provide education for various issues. That can mean educating clients or lawyers, but the education is a key component of the job. It's one that is often overlooked.

Jonathan: For me being a forensic social worker is about helping disenfranchised people get the most out of their rights. On the very basic human level, every person deserves a fair shot at being represented.

Children, for example, who need an advocate, will often be assigned a court-appointed person who looks out for their needs when they go through their court dates and to make sure that everything that needs to get done does. Forensic social workers work in conjunction with these advocates to make sure that the children are getting the services they need.

Adults also benefit from forensic social workers, say those who are working through a divorce. Custody disputes are often settled with the help of forensic social workers.

Q. What kind of degree do you have to have to become a forensic social worker?

Priscilla: I got a bachelor's degree in psychology with the intent of getting my master's degree in social work. Part of my bachelor's degree required me to have an internship, and I just happened to get one in a non-profit that dealt with legal issues. When I finished that, I volunteered in the legal aid office on campus. That inspired me to look into getting my law degree, which I did. After that, I practiced law for a year. I went back to get my master's degree in social work. I also have my certificate in forensic social work.

Jonathan: I have a bachelor's and a master's degree in social work with a certificate in forensic social work. It took me a total of six years to get my degrees, but I had the option of doing it through an accelerated program, but I took a semester off to work at an unpaid internship that didn't give me credit.

Q. What got you interested in forensic social work?

Priscilla: When I was doing my internship for my bachelor's degree I worked for a non-profit, and I shadowed one of their social workers. I remember one day in particular she had to go to court for a hearing to terminate parental rights. I never met the children, but she told me there were five of them. Both parents had been charged with criminal neglect. The house where the children were living was so filthy that it was condemned after the kids were taken. The parents didn't even show up for the hearing. The social worker I was shadowing was there to make sure that everyone's rights were represented. I just saw how much she cared about all of them. The kids and the parents. I knew at that moment that I wanted to do that, care about people for a living.

Jonathan: My story is a little different actually. When I was thirteen my parents went through a nasty divorce. There was a forensic social worker who helped me and my sister through the whole custody battle that ensued. She was the only stability we had at that point. My mom and dad were too caught up in their own drama and pain to help us.

It's because of her that I decided to become a social worker. I didn't know if I wanted to be a forensic social worker until I was in grad school. I thought I might want to do child welfare social work, but after talking to several people in that field, I worried that I'd get more frustrated with the red tape than anything else. Working as a forensic social worker, I'm able to help people through a particularly stressful time in their lives, and speak up for disenfranchised people.

Q. What is the best part about working in the legal system?

Priscilla: It's incredibly interesting. You work with so many different kinds of people on a daily basis that you never get bored. Most of my case load right now involves several child custody cases, and I have a few clients who are in juvenile detention. I like making a personal connection with my clients. Seeing them get the services they deserve and need is incredibly fulfilling.

Jonathan: I like working with a diverse array of people. It's been really rewarding to work with situations like the one I was in as a kid, and be for other kids what my social worker was for me. Sometimes all kids need is a familiar face, and there is always a moment with my clients when I realize that I have become that familiar person. If I could describe it, I would, but that look is what keeps me doing my job day after day.

Q. What's the hardest part about working in the legal system?

Priscilla: Definitely seeing all the cases with juveniles that have made such awful decisions. Those are the cases that break my heart. I want to fix them all.

Jonathan: For me the most difficult part of working in the legal system has been learning all the different laws and legal procedures. I didn't take any legal coursework per se, so it was all new to me when I started my job. I've definitely learned in the field, and I've done a lot of reading. When I get a case with things I don't understand I try to find as much information on the topic as I can. If reading isn't enough, I seek out the right professionals to answer my questions. The more informed I am, the better I can help my clients through what they are experiencing.

Q. What's your favorite part about your job?

Priscilla: Helping people figure out the confusing aspects of the legal system, and making sure that they get the services they need. The look of relief on a client's face when they realize that they understand what is going on around them or happening to them. It empowers them in a situation where they feel powerless. That's my favorite part of my job.

Jonathan: Honestly, I like providing stability for my clients. I'm a familiar face in unfamiliar territory. The relationship that you develop with a client when you are going through a difficult time with them is something that I can't adequately put into words, but you can see the difference you are making by the look on their faces when you walk into a room, and they recognize that they have an ally. Being the familiar face in a room of strangers is my favorite part of my job. I like to be able to build trust with my clients and make them feel calm under the circumstances.

Q. Do you have an area of specialization?

Priscilla: I wouldn't say I have an area of specialization, but I prefer to work with juvenile offenders. I feel like my legal background allows me to have a unique perspective as their social worker. Not only can I explain legal procedures and find them services, but I can also analyze their cases and give them advice that can help them formulate their own opinions and help them think of questions to ask. Because of my law degree, I'm often asked to take cases with complicated legal action happening. I like that because it makes me feel like I'm using all of my degrees together.

Jonathan: I feel like I specialize in child custody cases, though I work a variety of cases. Early in my career I asked for all of the child custody cases they would give me, so I've been able to hone my experience. I understand the legal side of child custody cases the best of any of the areas I work in too, so that helps me feel like that is my area of expertise. That has come from all my years of experience too, though. As I've said before I've had to do a lot of learning on the job.

Q. What is the most important part of your job?

Priscilla: I think the most important part of my job is demystifying the legal process so that my clients can make informed choices. There are so many factors that go into being involved in the legal system that addressing each of those areas is a necessity also.

Jonathan: For me the most important part of my job is providing stability and familiarity for my clients. I know I've said that before, but I believe that my role is to give my clients an ally so that they can focus on the other aspects of their cases.

Q. What's a case that stands out for you?

Priscilla: I had a case that involved a young girl, who I'll call Kylie. She was only fourteen years old, but she'd been caught selling marijuana at school. She swore she was only holding it for her boyfriend, but, of course, the boyfriend denied everything.

Kylie ended up in a juvenile detention center while she waited for her case to be heard, and while she was there her mother was arrested on a drug charge. Kylie didn't have any other family who could be named her guardian, so she became a ward of the state. She was assigned a child welfare social worker, and in turn, her social worker contacted our organization. I was assigned to her case. She needed someone to be with her during all of her legal proceedings. Her other social worker was there also, but I was going to be her guide.

The reason the case stands out is that so many things went wrong and made it more complicated. It was also one of my first solo cases, so it was one of the first that I really threw myself into wholeheartedly.

Right before her first court date, another charge was brought against her. Her boyfriend had been arrested during a home break-in. It turned out that he'd been doing that quite often, and Kylie had been with him during several of the robberies. So she now had another case against her.

I went with her to her meetings with the public defender and explained all the legal terms and implications to her. She readily admitted her involvement in the robberies, but continued to deny the drug charges, so I was inclined to believe her.

What struck me most about her was that she was such a quiet girl. She kept to herself and didn't cause any trouble at the juvenile detention center. She went to her classes. I had a hard time believing that she would have been in on the robberies, but she gave us all kinds of details that her boyfriend had also given the police. Looking back, I think the biggest thing about myself at that time was that I wanted to be the one to save her. That wasn't my job. That wasn't the focus of my job, but that's what I wanted.

I made weekly visits to her at juvie to update her on the progress of her cases. The drug charge was eventually dropped, but she was convicted as an accessory to armed robbery. She was sentenced to a few months more in the juvenile detention center, and then she'd get probation until she was eighteen. I laid out what that meant for her, and I really thought that she understood how she could get her life together.

That was my own ego. I think that because I had spent so much time with her that I thought I had influenced her to want to do well, do better with her life. Yes, she'd made a mistake, made a bad choice for companions, but that didn't have to define her. What I didn't take into account was that before she got into trouble her life was falling apart. Her mother was addicted to a variety of drugs, selling them on the side to feed her habit, and she turned to the first guy who showed interest in her.

I made sure that I stayed up to date on her case as she served out her time and was released to a group home. After that I had no connection with her case, although I did keep in contact with her child welfare worker. Because I had already sunk myself so deep into her case, I really felt like I needed to keep in the loop. Professionally that wasn't the wisest move, of course, but emotionally it taught me so much about my job, and what I was meant to do.

About a year later, Kylie was arrested again on prostitution charges. I asked to be assigned to her case, and because I had already worked with her, they allowed me to take the case. When I met with her I was surprised that she didn't remember me because we had spent so much time together. I was more mature that time around, though, and I knew not to take it personally. That was a hard distinction for me to make, but I'm glad that I was able to learn it.

That time through I made sure that Kylie knew all the things that were happening, and what each thing meant, just like I had before. After her first court date we found out that she was pregnant, and she wanted to keep the baby. Her new child welfare worker was pushing for her to give the baby up for adoption because she knew that once Kylie had the baby that kid would be put into foster care. The public defender never made any promises to Kylie that she'd get off. If anything every time we met with Kylie's lawyer there was a lot of cautioning that she'd be going to jail again. Once she was in jail there was no way that she could keep her baby with her, and after she got out it would be much harder for her to get her child back. Unless she cleaned up her life completely.

Kylie did go to jail again, but I was able to make sure that when she went to a different juvenile detention center that she got services she needed. Things like therapy and job training. I knew that with those things she at least had a shot at turning her life around, whereas the first time through I thought that I could help her just by my interest in her and her life. I did my job the first time, but I didn't actually do my job. That's a weird thing to say, but it's the way I learned how to actually determine what my clients need.

Jonathan: I'm going to sound like a total cliché, but the case that has always stood out to me the most is the first one where I got to be in the role that my social worker was for me.

The case was eerily similar to my own parents' divorce. The mother had filed for divorce after the father had an affair, and the whole thing was acrimonious. Both of them were completely unfriendly to me, and I wonder if my own parents were that way to the social worker who helped us.

There was a boy and a girl, both older than me and my sister, but their pain reminded me so much of my own at that point in the divorce. The girl was outright hostile toward her father, so one of the first things I made sure that I did was find a support group for her near her school. That wasn't explicitly a part of my job, but I feel like the more services we can offer, especially for kids, the better shot they have at getting through the event without too much trauma.

I found that my perspective from the other side of the table was pretty much what I thought it would be. The first time I met with the kids was when they were being interviewed for the custody proceedings. They were both asked various questions about what was going on at home and who they would prefer to live with. Both the kids chose their mom, but the boy was conflicted. I remember feeling that way too, and I told him that. I remember feeling like I was somehow being disloyal to my dad by choosing my mom, even though it was my dad's choices that were destroying our family. Of course, as a kid, I didn't know how to articulate that perspective so I just let it eat me up inside.

Having gone through that experience myself, I was able to connect with both of my clients in a way that I wouldn't have been able to without it. So I've always been grateful for that experience.

I think a lot of people have a negative connotation with social workers, and that's a problem because, really, we're here to help. After that first custody case, I've had about a dozen others. I guess our agency thinks they're my specialty. Not that I mind. What I've noticed is that a lot of the kids are really reluctant to talk to me when they first meet me, even though I'm not the one asking questions. At the first meeting I'm generally just there for support and to explain proceedings to the kids so we're sure they understand. I'm also there to represent their rights in the process because they often don't have a voice.

From what some of the kids have told me they're usually afraid to talk in front of me because they're worried that I'll take them away from their parents and put them in foster care. I've never been at custody and divorce proceedings where abuse or neglect is found. I'm sure that does happen in some cases, but not in mine. I explain how my role is different from that of other social workers, and that I'm there primarily for their benefit.

That first case really stands out for me, though, because I got to move into the role that had made such a difference in my childhood. I really credit our social worker for giving me the stability I needed at a time I needed it the most so that I could focus on growing up. I didn't get mired in anger and fear. I knew that I had an adult in my life who would be there when I needed her. And she was there, it seemed, until my parents got their act together.

Kids aren't very well-equipped to deal with their parents' drama. People always say how resilient kids are, and that's true. I've seen that time and again, but they also do that to cope and survive. Being resilient doesn't mean that they can have tons of turmoil dumped on them just because they'll deal with it. That's another part of my job that I like, being able to help them sort through the stuff they've been dealt, and getting it into more manageable pieces.

Another thing that case helped me realize is just how much pain both my parents were in during the divorce, so in a sense it helped me heal some old hurts as well. That's not part of my job obviously, but it's a bonus. I've gone to several seminars on using your life experience to make you a better social worker. I'm not sure how I'd say I fair in the other areas of my job, probably fair to middling, but I know I excel at the custody cases.

I still think about those kids in that first case. That was almost ten years ago, so both of them would be in their twenties by now.

They're adults. That kind of blows my mind when I let myself think about it. I helped kids who grew up. Sometimes I wonder if they think about me the way I think about my social worker. Them or any of the kids I've helped.

That's the hardest part about my job. You don't get immediate feedback, if you get it at all. Most of the time you are helping people in the middle of emotional turmoil, so you end up seeing them at their most vulnerable. I've had many clients thank me for the work I've done for them, and that always feels great. When doesn't it? But it's not about that for me. Accolades make you feel good for a moment, but it's so much better when I look back over the last ten years and think about all of the hard work that I've done to make people's lives better, easier.

Q. What advice do you have for someone thinking about working in the forensic social work field?

Priscilla: I think that forensic social work is the least known and least understood area of social work, so I fully encourage anyone looking at a social work degree to find out more about this field. Most schools will have guidance counselors who can tell you about what the school offers or where to get the certificate you are interested in.

I also think that internships are the most valuable asset you have as a student. I actually wish I had done a few more internships before I graduated. I think that you can find out so much about the field by shadowing people who already work in that field. Not only can you see real-world applications of the things you learn in class, but sometimes the organizations and people you work with give you actual work to do so you can learn in the field.

So my advice is that you should consider the field of forensic social work because you have the chance to help an underserved population. You can make such a difference in an area that often

67

confuses and scares people, and there's such a variety that you'll never get bored.

Jonathan: My advice is to find out as much about each part of forensic social work as you can because once you get into the field, there will be all sorts of things that surprise you. You'll think that you learned everything during your degree or certificate program, including all of the possible solutions to each problem that might arise. And what you find out is that you are dead wrong. You will feel like you've learned virtually nothing and wonder what you paid all that money for.

The reason for that, I think, is because the real world isn't as neat and clean as a textbook. Even case studies have been written up by someone to make a point. The best teacher I've had is experience. Internships are a great way of learning in the field while you are still in school, but learning on the job is an inevitability. You have to be prepared to go above and beyond your job description and often need to look for creative solutions to problems that present themselves.

I think that forensic social work is a great field, and I encourage everyone who is in a social work program to look into this field.

Bonus Section: Five Life Hacks for Social Workers

Life Hack #1: Find apps for your phone that can make your life easier.

Using apps can condense the amount of stuff you need to take with you when you have to be out of the office. Apps can also be used as distraction for children in the case of child welfare or school social work. Making a list of the important parts of your job can give you ideas for what to search for. If you work in the medical, substance abuse, or mental health field, there are a number of apps that deal with behavior and medication tracking. If you work in the child welfare or school social work field, you might find it helpful to have apps on your phone that can distract and entertain kids as well as apps that can generate discussion.

Here are five to get you started:

1. Social Work Master's Exam Prep, $4.99 on itunes.

   (https://itunes.apple.com/us/app/social-work-masters-exam-prep/id453540673?mt=8)

   This app does exactly what it sounds like; it helps you prepare for your master's exam. Especially helpful for studying on the go. There is a study mode and a test mode to ensure that you are more than ready for your big test.

2. Depressioncheck, free on itunes

   (https://itunes.apple.com/us/app/depressioncheck/id398170644?mt=8)

This app is pretty straight forward, but is extremely useful in the assessment of patients, especially in a community health or school setting. The app leads users through a short, three minute checklist that helps to assess the patient's risk for depression and a number of other anxiety disorders.

3. How Would You Feel If...Fun Deck, $3.99 on itunes.

(https://itunes.apple.com/us/app/how-would-you-feel-if-.../id459752073?mt=8)

This app leads the user through a series of scenarios, allowing the user to choose how he or she feels about each. This app would be good as means of starting conversations with kids. One example given on the app's page is, "How would you feel if you got lost at the mall?" The child then presses the red or the green button indicating a positive or negative feeling. The discussions could be used as springboards to other topics.

4. Camscanner Free, free on itunes.

(https://itunes.apple.com/us/app/camscanner-free/id388627783?mt=8)

This app is designed for scanning documents. A social worker who works in a field that involves home visits or visits to facilities would find this useful. This can help a social worker to obtain important documentation that might otherwise take much longer to obtain.

5. Touch and Learn—Emotions, free on itunes.

(https://itunes.apple.com/us/app/touch-and-learn-emotions/id451685022?mt=8)

This is a simple, but powerful app that can be useful when working with children. Each screen shows four pictures, and the child is asked to find the one that corresponds to the word on the screen (examples include smiling, sad, etc.) This app can be used to generate conversations with children as well as adults.

Life Hack #2: Read stories (novels, memoirs, guides) from your field.

Not only is reading a good way to de-stress, but it can also give you good perspective on subjects that you have never personally encountered. The following are six books (both fiction and nonfiction) to give you a jumping off point.

1. *A Trick of the Light* by Lois Metzger

   (http://www.amazon.com/Trick-Light-Lois-Metzger/dp/0062133098/ref=sr_1_2?ie=UTF8&qid=1424658395&sr=8-2&keywords=a+trick+of+the+light)

   This story is narrated by a teenage boy with anorexia. Boys are a minority when it comes to eating disorders, which is certainly a perfect reason to read this book. Anyone working with teens could benefit from this book.

2. *Skin and Bones* by Sherry Shahan

   (http://www.amazon.com/Skin-Bones-Sherry-Shahan/dp/0807573973/ref=pd_sim_sbs_b_17?ie=UTF8&refRID=1MHRNCCEKJV9Y3N1MVWK)

71

This novel is about a boy in treatment for an eating disorder and the people he meets while in treatment. This book deals with the struggle to get well, and the choices that affect that struggle. Clearly, while it is fiction, the story gives a good view of what goes on inside a teen's mind in treatment. A good read for people interested in working with teens or in treatment facilities.

3. *Double Double* by Martha and Ken Grimes

   (http://www.amazon.com/Double-Dual-Memoir-Alcoholism/dp/1476724083/ref=sr_1_2?s=books&ie=UTF8&qid=1424658915&sr=1-2&keywords=Double+Double)

   This memoir deals with the road to recovery from alcoholism of a mother and son. This story delves into addiction from a very intimate point of view. It also deals with hereditary issues and codependence.

4. *Three Little Words* by Ashley Rhodes-Courter

   (http://www.amazon.com/Three-Little-Words-A-Memoir/dp/1416948074/ref=pd_sim_b_5?ie=UTF8&refRID=0A2878FJBCW841QD99E2)

   This book deals with the painful childhood of a girl who went through 14 foster homes in nine years. This book sheds light on a broken foster system and can help someone wanting to learn more about a career in child welfare social work from the perspective of the child.

5. *To The End of June* by Cris Beam

(http://www.amazon.com/To-End-June-Intimate-American/dp/0544103440/ref=pd_sim_b_6?ie=UTF8&refRID=0CV1TX8C3HDAVE4R9DMF)

This book deals again with the broken foster care system, but especially about what happens to kids when they age out of foster care. The book is brutally honest and would be useful for anyone interested in child welfare social work.

6. *Being Mortal* by Atul Gawande

(http://www.amazon.com/Being-Mortal-Medicine-What-Matters/dp/0805095152/ref=sr_1_1?s=books&ie=UTF8&qid=1424659727&sr=1-1&keywords=being+mortal)

Atul Gawande is a surgeon who deals with the limitations of his profession by creating an environment where patients and their families can get the best quality of life possible. By highlighting these shortcomings, he is able to suggest a new path, one that lifts everyone to a better place no matter what their circumstances. This book should be a must read for anyone interested in medical social work.

Life Hack #3: Use ordinary board games in therapy to generate discussion in a non-threatening way.

1. Jenga

You can use the bricks to talk about any number of things. While building the tower you can talk about ways that we build up situations in our lives until they can seem overwhelming. Or you can use the building up language to encourage those in the group to talk about good things that have happened to them in the past week.

Each time someone moves a brick, they can answer a predetermined question, from mundane (What's the best thing about winter?) to the in-depth (How do you feel when your best friend says something mean to you?) You could also write the questions directly on the bricks so that the person would just read the question as they moved the piece.

When the tower ultimately falls, this can be used as a symbolic fall that everyone experiences. It can be a jumping-off point to talk about the lows that were experienced during the week, struggles, or simply stumbling blocks.

2. Candy Land

This game works especially well with young children who aren't literate. Like the Jenga blocks, the different color cards can be used to generate conversation. Each time a purple card is drawn, for example, everyone can share their favorite book or movie or games.

With each round of cards drawn, the questions can become more thought provoking and discussion building. This technique would work well for settings where group therapy is utilized, although it could certainly be used for one on one therapy sessions as well.

The characters from Candy Land can also be used to discuss the people in their lives. For example, the characters that we perceive as good could be used to generate discussion about the good people in their lives. The same could be done for the bad characters.

There is also the way Candy Land takes the players on a journey. If appropriate, the board could be used as an analogy for the journey each child is taking toward recovery. The game starts out in a place that seems super far away from the castle at the end. Throughout the game, players must pass through darkness and can face setbacks, but ultimately they arrive at the castle. Even when the road to recovery seems long and the person faces setbacks, they will eventually reach their goal if they continue moving forward.

3. Life

The game of Life deals with all the milestones that generally happen in a person's life. Graduating, getting a job, getting married, having kids, etc., are among the things that happen over the course of the game.

This is a good game to get kids talking about where they see themselves in the future. If there are stumbling blocks, such as not seeing themselves getting a degree or getting married or having kids, there might be reasons hidden in their lack of answers.

The novelty of the game can distract from the awkwardness of sharing their innermost thoughts and help them to feel comfortable opening up in a strange environment. As with Candy Land, the journey aspect of the game could be used to talk about the journey through recovery.

All of the above-mentioned games are just examples of games that could be used to generate discussion. Any game, but especially board games, can be adaptable to this method. And there are certainly plenty of options for kids of all ages.

Life Hack #4: Recommend these movies to people when they want to know what you do or start spouting clichés at you.

1. *It Takes Two*. The movie is a story about two little girls, one a wealthy child and the other a foster kid. The two meet in the woods near a camp for foster kids and the wealthy child's home. They decide to switch places to see how the other one lives. The single father of the wealthy child and the social worker in charge of the foster child eventually fall in love.

   Sound cheesy? Maybe a little, but what makes this movie so great is the portrayal of the social worker. She's not paid much, but she does her job with her whole being. She loves the children in her care and fights hard to keep them safe, even when the system decides otherwise.

2. *Lilo and Stitch*. Another children's movie, but one that's even more accessible as it's a Disney movie. The plot revolves around a little girl named Lilo who lives with her older sister after their parents die. In the movie, they adopt a "dog" who turns out to be an alien. In the end everyone gets a warm, fuzzy feeling

when family is shown to be the most important thing of all.

What makes this movie a good watch for people in the social work field or to recommend to others is that it reminds everyone that families are worth keeping together if possible, and that families don't always look like everyone's idea of a family. These non-traditional family units don't diminish the realness or importance of that family.

The social worker in this movie, Cobra Bubbles, is a tough man who constantly seems to show up at the worst possible moments. He eventually deems it necessary to move Lilo to a foster home, but changes his mind after a series of events shows him that her sister can take care of her safely. Despite his gruff exterior, Mr. Bubbles really does care about Lilo and her sister, and he wants to do what is best for both of them.

3. *Girl, Interrupted.* This movie revolves around a teenager who is admitted to a psychiatric hospital after an attempted suicide. She meets a group of girls who have a range of issues including depression, eating disorders, and OCD.

   While this movie doesn't deal with social work directly, it does deal with a wide array of mental health issues that a mental health care social worker could encounter, especially in a treatment facility. This is a good movie to encourage empathy for those dealing with mental illness.

The movie also serves as a reminder of the complexity of dealing with mental illness and how often women are diagnosed with things like depression and eating disorders. While the movie follows a group of teenage girls, the problems presented in the movie affect a wide range of ages, genders, races, and socioeconomic statuses.

4. *I Am Sam*. This movie follows the story of a developmentally disabled father as he tries to secure his parental rights to his daughter after her mother abandoned her. This movie deals with the legal aspects of child custody cases, which a forensic social worker would deal with, as well as the placement of the child in a foster home, which involves child welfare social workers.

   This movie also deals with the prejudices that are present against parents with disabilities in the legal system. It also provides a view of foster care and fostering with the intent to adopt. There is a compassionate response from the foster family to the child and father's situation, and this can serve as a good example of how birth and foster families can work together for the best interest of the child.

5. *Precious*. This movie follows the life of an abused teenager named Precious. Pregnant with her second child by her father, Precious struggles in school until an observant principal sends her to an alternative school. After she connects with her new teacher,

Precious begins to learn to read and write. As she befriends other students, her confidence grows. With the support of her new friends, her teacher, and her social worker, Precious is able to gain control of her life, and move forward for the sake of her two children.

This movie shows a social worker who has a heavy case load, but sincerely cares about her cases. The social worker struggles to help Precious as much as she needs to, but remains supportive of the girl as much as she can.

This movie is a good example of what positive support can do for an at-risk youth. While the outcome isn't a typical happily ever after, it is a happy ending, or maybe more importantly, a happy beginning. This movie shows the importance of not letting at-risk youth fall through the cracks. It also shows how schools and social workers can work together to provide care for students. There is also a good example of how poverty affects people and the choices that they make.

Life Hack #5: Create a therapy bag with easy to take along items.

While many sources suggest having a therapy bag for all kinds of social work situations, the benefit of having one, particularly when working with kids, can't be stressed enough. When you have something that can distract kids from the stress of the current situation, you will be able to perform your job better and more effectively. The following are six items that could easily be thrown into a purse or back pack.

1. Small jars of Play-Doh. Tossing a few colors of this stuff into a therapy bag can work wonders for kids who have to wait for anything, or for kids who need to be distracted from the circumstances going on around them. The repetition of smashing the soft dough can act like a stress ball and help calm children down. They are sold in small tubs so it's relatively easy to find a variety of colors, and they don't take up much space in the bag, allowing for you to keep several handy.

2. Small bag of candy. Suggestions would be either something like a small chocolate or a hard candy, though that can be a choking hazard for small kids. Candy can be a quick pick me up for a distressed child who is already tired and hungry. Candy is also a good treat that can help put a child at ease. Again this is a small item that can make a big impact. Taking care of a child's hunger can also assuage the more complicated aspect of emotional distress.

3. Toy cell phone, preferably one that makes noise or lights up. This sounds like an odd item, but especially for young children, the novelty of a cell phone, even a toy, can help distract them from what's going on. This can also be good for therapy as the child can pretend to call their parents or others that they need to call. This can help the child feel in control of a situation in which they have virtually no control. Being another small item, this is a good one to include.

4. An I Spy jar. This is a small jar filled with rice and little toys. The child shakes or rolls the jar to move the rice around and tries to see how many different things they can find. This is a good time-filling toy. It is also a good toy to use between social worker and child. Playing an actual game of I Spy together can break the ice and get the child comfortable with a stranger that has turned their world upside down.

5. A teddy bear. The ultimate comfort item. You can get a smallish bear for a reasonable price. When a child has been taken away from everything familiar, having a small stuffed animal to cuddle can be extremely helpful. If you are able to give a bear to each child you have in your case load that can be a nice gesture, but it's enough to simply have the bear in your therapy bag. Knowing what to say to a child that has just been removed from a bad situation can be next to impossible, but a teddy bear can often help.

6. A small container full of dominoes. Dominoes can double as blocks and are a great distraction. Dominoes are also good for school social workers who need to have something for their students to do while they wait.

Bibliography:

http://en.wikipedia.org/wiki/Medical_social_work

http://healthcareers.about.com/od/healthcareerprofiles/p/MedSoc
Work.htm

http://www.socialworklicensure.org/types-of-social-
workers/medical-health-social-worker.html

http://www.thebestschools.org/blog/2012/04/16/25-master-social-
work-degree-programs/

http://msw.wustl.edu/your-msw/

http://swadmissions.columbia.edu/frequently-asked-questions-
online-campus/

http://www.allpsychologycareers.com/career/substance-abuse-
social-worker.html

http://socialworkdegreesonline.net/substance-abuse-social-
workers.html

http://www.socialworkweb.com/nasw/choose/substance_abuse.cf
m

http://www.dcccd.edu/CD/DCC/Health/SocialWork/about/Pages/
degrees.aspx

http://careersinpsychology.org/start-a-mental-health-social-work-
career/

http://msw.usc.edu/academic/concentrations/mental-health/

http://ssw.umich.edu/programs/msw/overview/mental-health

http://socialworkdegreesonline.net/child-welfare-social-workers.html

http://online.aurora.edu/my/bachelor-social-work/?plc={placement}&utm_source=bing&utm_medium=PPC&utm_campaign=~%5BS%5D+BA+Social+Work_Social_Work_Modified&utm_content=7184768567&utm_term=a%20social%20work%20degree&tid=50d0d4fd3b8e1&mkwid=elLLsebe_dc&pcrid=7184768567&pkw=a%20social%20work%20degree&pmt=bp

http://jobs.newsok.com/jobs/child-welfare-specialist-3-livingston-la-75474219-d?networkView=national

http://www.socialwork.pitt.edu/researchtraining/child-welfare-ed-research-programs/children-youth-families-certificate

http://en.wikipedia.org/wiki/Forensic_social_work

http://study.com/articles/Forensic_Social_Work_Certificate_Program_Overview.html

http://nofsw.org/?page_id=10

http://www.ehow.com/info_7791570_salary-forensic-social-worker.html

http://www.abfsw.us/

http://www.acfei.com/forensic_membership/

http://www.forensictraininginstitute.org/?Online_Certification_Courses:Certification_Courses_Offered:Certified_Forensic_Social_Worker

http://socialworkdegreesonline.net/social-work-bachelors-degree-in-minnesota.html

http://www.cosw.sc.edu/academic-program

http://sowkweb.usc.edu/master-of-social-work/msw-degree/dual-degrees

Lightning Source UK Ltd.
Milton Keynes UK
UKHW020904240223
417581UK00010B/961